A Way of Being

A Way of Being

by David Cadman

ZIG Publishing

This essay is based upon a text originally submitted to
The Friends Quarterly competition in 2009, parts of which
may be published by *The Friends Quarterly* as an anthology.

Published by ZIG Publishing,
The Box House, Priors Way,
Aldeburgh. IP15 5EW.

September 2010

ISBN: 978-0-9566900-0-5

Printed by Fuller Davies Ltd., Ipswich

To Miriam of Magdala

Acknowledgements

I would like to thank and acknowledge: Jules Cashford, Joseph Milne and Father Silouan for their guidance and teaching; Barbara Pensom for her critical and grounded comment; and Kim Samuel for her generous and kind support.

Thank you also to Marchela Dimitrova for her beautiful icon which appears on the cover of this book; and to David Gillingwater of Herring Bone Design for his part in bringing this book into being.

Walking with companions is so much better than walking alone.

Contents

Introduction

"So all things tend through their movements and actions toward the divine likeness, as towards their ultimate end."

Thomas Aquinas.[1]

All is one. The material world is at the same time the field of mysticism – the union of the mind and heart with the eternal reality underlying all that exists, the ultimate fulfilment of the love of Truth. The mundane and the divine are one. What may at first seem to be realms separate and apart are, in truth, so interdependent that the one cannot be understood, or even spoken of, without the other. Thus, if we seek Truth, we cannot discuss any matter, however mundane, other than in a language that brings us to a Oneness of Being, a way of being that draws us into union with the Great Mystery, The Divine.

As Quakers, we know this to be true and reflect it in the way we are. Our business meetings begin with silence and stillness; and our worship leads to practical action in our everyday lives. But beyond this, the compelling convention of our time is to separate and divide; and sometimes we allow this to take over our thoughts and words, in such a way that, almost unknowingly, we, too, separate everyday matters from divine discourse. In doing this, we not only deny our faith but also fail to see clearly. We lose our way.

This is especially so in the realm of economy – the "divine realm" of secular modernism, with its own creed of unquestionable truths. Indeed, the power of its priesthood is such that, despite all the evidence of disarray, it remains difficult even to ask questions without

---

[1] Thomas Aquinas, *Summa Contra Gentiles*, Book 3 Part 1, 19.5, translated by Anton Pegis, 1973.

being accused of mischief or impertinence or both. But if the king has no clothes on, some poor child must say this is so. To be true to our faith, we must at least be prepared to ask questions; for unless and until we do so, we shall be unable to find our way through to a form of economy that is at one with The Divine.

Our present Western (and increasingly Eastern) model of economy is based upon the common presumption that the greatest good for the greatest many comes from a form of economy in which we are encouraged evermore to increase our consumption of goods and services. This self-concern is supposed to cause a "trickle down" of wealth so that the poorest benefit as much as the rich — a win for everybody. To achieve this, our economy is dependent upon, addicted to, "growth". But, although this addiction continues, and is espoused by politicians of all kinds, the truth is, the model is not only deeply flawed but leads us, and others, into greater and greater distress.[2]

This is not a simple matter nor should it be assumed that a model of no-growth would be some sort of panacea. Nevertheless, our particular model of growth is full of shortcomings. What is taken into account in the measurement of growth is partial and excludes all sorts of activities such as childcare and neighbourliness. It does not take account of the costs of growth, which include not only personal/social stress but also material factors such as resource depletion, the loss of topsoils, the degradation of fish stocks and the long run emission of carbon into the atmosphere. In mature economies, continuing economic growth does not deliver commensurate and continuing growth in measures of well-being or life satisfaction;[3] and there is plenty of evidence to show that it does

---

[2] David Cadman, "Limits to Growth", *Quaker Voices, Vol. 5*, September 2010
[3] See for example Shah H and Marks N, *A well-being manifesto for a flourishing society*, New Economics Foundation, London, 2004; the work of the Pembina Institute, Alberta Genuine Progress Indicator, Centennial Update 2005, Alberta, Canada; and Eduardo Lora and Juan Camilo Chaparro, *The Conflictive Relationship Between Satisfaction and Income*, Inter-American Development Bank, 2008.

not reduce the gap between the rich and the poor. Finally, as we now know, our addiction to growth has been propped up by unsustainable levels of debt – something that our children will be paying for many years to come.

Facing up to this problem is not easy, since the root perception upon which it is based is deeply embedded in modern conventions; and those that speak with the voice of convention seldom have to justify their opinion – they assume it is taken for granted. Despite all the evidence to contrary, convention tells us this kind of growth, what I want to call "old growth", is the answer to all our woes, not their cause; that by some sort of magic, the greatest good for us all will come about from our individual selfishness – our relentless quest to have more. Accepting that for the goodness of the whole we have to live within limits just does not fit this old model. For this understanding to arise in us, a radical change of heart and mind is required. A transformation of the language of economy is needed.

For something like 350 years, our lives and our understanding of what is or, indeed, can be considered to be true or real has been shaped almost exclusively by an unbalanced, reductive and materialist rationality. Beginning with The Age of Reason and then The Enlightenment, this mode of rationality has encouraged us to see things as separate and apart. And although we are now, once more, beginning to see the interconnectedness of all that is – for example in our concern with environment and ecology or with integrated health care – this rather narrow, particular but outmoded way of thinking still holds us in its thrall. Although we are now beginning to see that being is always "being-in-relationship" – or as I would say relating-ness – it still requires conscious effort and discipline for us to shun the damaging propaganda of what I sense will soon be known as "the old time". For this old time mistakenly describes a world unerringly riven with competition and strife, where, by looking out for our own advantage, we will miraculously contribute to the good of all.

In coming to terms with the challenge of climate change and limits to growth, and in answering anew the question of who is my neighbour, we will have to break free from the bounds of this old, fractured and insufficient world; for otherwise, whether or not we are Quakers, our ability to see what might be possible will be mightily constrained and diminished, and our vision for the future will be blinkered. We shall find ourselves, like the politicians at the 2009 Copenhagen summit, fettered by old ways and by an old language.

This being so, it is important to remember that, despite our inheritance, there was "a time before", a time when the understanding of one-ness was commonplace; when seeing the world as whole and interconnected seemed obvious and natural; when justice was seen to be part of our natural participation in the goodness of being. This was not some Golden Age of perfection but just another time. Midst all its own difficulties, injustices and unhappiness, this was a time when the experience of wholeness was simply common, the experience of the everyday. In the traditional and sacred mythology of all peoples, it has always been there.

I want to propose, then, that we need, once more, to reclaim this notion of wholeness or "holiness" as part of our everyday lives *now*; to suggest that without this common experience and remembrance something will always be missing; to suggest that the absence of wholeness and holiness leaves us incomplete and empty both within ourselves and with neighbours near and far. I do not know how we can find the right way forward, the right way to *be* together, but I do know this will not be possible unless and until we are able to dwell within and become part of such holiness, to find a way of being that unites us with Divine Presence.

A Common Understanding

"The blinkers worn by Englishmen enable them to trot all the more steadily along the beaten road, without being disturbed by curiosity as to their destination."

R. H. Tawney.[4]

Beneath a calm surface, there has always been in our Society of Friends a fervent questing for truth and direction. And although the underlying structure of our meetings for worship and our business meetings continue to follow simple and traditional principles of silence and inclusion, British Quakers have never been locked into rigid forms of practise. There has always been plenty of discussion of, and disagreement about, social and political issues. There has been, too, a richness of work beyond the Meeting House. If, in my lifetime, peace testimony and a marked concern for global poverty have been especially strong, there have also been many other matters that have engaged the attention and effort of Friends. Most recently, this has meant a growing concern for sustainability and climate change, for living within our means and within the limits of Nature – for our sakes and for the sake of all who live or may come to live on planet Earth.

There has also been discussion about what it means to be a Quaker, or, rather, what it means to "be Quaker".[5] If this raises questions about having and being, it also raises questions about the place of theology and action in our testimony. For some of us, perhaps all of us, theology and action cannot be considered apart. Both are part of

[4] R. H. Tawney, *The Acquisitive Society*, 1921.
[5] Elaine Pryce, "Being Quaker: the lost heritage of Quietist spirituality", *The Friends Quarterly*, January 2008, 7-16.

"being Quaker" and there is a danger in supposing otherwise – a separation of principle and action, of means and ends, which can sometimes lead us astray. True action is founded on true contemplation and prayer. Theology has no meaning other than in respect to the work of life, however it might be defined. Nevertheless, it is not uncommon for such a separation to occur; those most active and concerned with work have no time for theological reflection and those taken up with theology lack any sense of how it might be expressed in the everyday. And these lapses into disconection are reinforced by a powerful, if outmoded, convention, a powerful but now outmoded worldview.

For a very long time, our lives and our understanding of what can be considered to be true or real have been shaped almost exclusively by that unbalanced, narrow, reductive and materialist rationality to which I have already referred. This has encouraged us to see things separate and apart. In his book *The Acquisitive Society*, written in the early part of the twentieth century R. H. Tawney puts it as follows:

> The natural consequence of the abdication of authorities which had stood, however imperfectly, for a common purpose in social organization, was the gradual disappearance from social thought of the idea of purpose itself. Its place in the eighteenth century was taken by the idea of mechanism. The conception of men as united to each other, and of all mankind as united to God, by mutual obligations arising from their common end, ceased to be impressed upon men's minds, when Church and State withdrew from the centre of social life to its circumference. Vaguely conceived and imperfectly realized, it had been the keystone holding together the social fabric. What remained when the keystone of the arch was removed was private rights and private interests, the materials of a society, rather than a society itself.[6]

---

[6] R. H. Tawney, *The Acquisitive Society*, Victor Gollanz Limited, 1937, 18. First published in 1921.

This became our world. But as I have said in my Introduction, we must now break free from its fetters and reclaim a notion of wholeness or "holiness" as part of *our* everyday lives. For without this common experience and remembrance something is missing. The absence of wholeness and holiness leaves us incomplete, our sight obscured.

Reflecting on all of this, and looking for a way of being that is whole and holy, I have stumbled upon two teachings that I would like to share with you. The first is found in *The Gospel of Mary Magdalene* and the second is found in the writings of the thirteenth century monk, Thomas Aquinas, and his teaching of what is called "Natural Law".

First, Mary Magdalene...

Nature is expressed in pattern, order and rhythm. We live within this regularity and are a part of it. It is so familiar to us we seldom notice it. And yet we would be surprised if our inward breath did not follow our out-breath; if morning did not follow day or springtime follow winter; if the ebb-tide did not follow its flow. We expect the sun to rise in the East and set in the West; and we expect the moon to grow, become full and decline into darkness before arising again. Within these patterns, within this regularity, we too arise and decline, and I take this as my frame of reference – for whatever else is unknown, I know this to be true.

Although this idea of a natural and intrinsic order or lawfulness in all things has ancient roots, its meaning has been lost. This is how the scholar Joseph Milne[7] puts it:

> The modern notion of law means general principles which determine things from outside themselves. ...The ancient conception of law is quite different from this. It means the "essence" or "nature" of a thing. Thus the law of anything is its mode of being and its manner in participating among the many things of the cosmos and in being as such.[8]

According to this teaching, order and purposefulness arise from within as a yearning for the goodness of the whole and can only be found in the "mode of being" – a way of being. This is what our forebears called Wisdom.

The qualities of Wisdom are sometimes differentiated from the qualities of Law – the one inward, integrative and participative and the other outward, separating and authoritative. But care has to be taken lest these distinctions become overly divisive, implying that the two are ever-opposed one to another. The truth is that, although at any one time the balance between the two may be disturbed, both are necessary parts of a whole. We need, therefore, to understand what happens when the balance between them is disturbed, when Law becomes overly external, mechanistic and oppressive and when the integrative and nurturing voice of Wisdom is lost. Indeed, I want to suggest that as a religious community rooted in mysticism rather than dogma we, as Quakers, have a special responsibility to restore a better harmony between these two, so that they may once again be One.

---

[7] Joseph Milne is a writer and scholar and a Fellow of The Temenos Academy.
[8] Joseph Milne, *Natural Law and Ecology*, a paper given to the Henry George Foundation, February 2010.

Within the canonical gospels, it is difficult to find teachings that speak of the wholeness of all that is, although the parable of the Vine talks about our union with the Divine:

I am the vine, ye are the branches: He that abideth in me, and I in him, the same bringeth forth much fruit: for without me ye can do nothing.[9]

But within the gnostic gospels it is there. Here it is in the relatively well-known *Gospel of Thomas*:

When you make the two One,
and you make the inner even as the outer,
and the outer even as the inner
and the above even as the below,
so that you will make the male and female
into a single One,
in order that the male is not made male
nor female made female...
Then you shall enter the kingdom of heaven.[10]

But, most especially, it is there in *The Gospel of Mary Magdalene*, the first extant verses of which plunge us into a realm of wonderment and integration.

---

[9] John 15 1-27.

[10] *The Gospel of Thomas*, presented by Hugh McGregor Ross, William Sessions Limited, The Ebor Press, York, 1987, Login 22.

The Teacher [Jesus] answered:
"All that is born, all that is created,
all the elements of Nature
are interwoven and united with each other.
All that is composed shall be decomposed;
everything returns to its roots;
matter returns to the origin of matter.
Those who have ears, let them hear."[11]

This teaching is important for us now, as it is the lost voice of Wisdom, which speaks of those qualities of integration and continuity without which there can be no Union.

But who is this Mary Magdalene who speaks to us and why should we heed what she has to say? Because the picture is unclear, we can only find answers to this question by opening our hearts, waiting and, as it were, allowing her to speak to us. From the cloud of uncertainty some clarity shines through: she was especially loved by Jesus and washed his feet with her tears, drying them with her hair; Jesus purified her spirit so that she could see clearly[12] and just before his betrayal, she anointed his head with oil; she was there at the foot of the cross; wept for him and came to his tomb with sweet spices, before being the first to see the risen Christ; and she was the one who received special teachings, with an instruction to take them to the other disciples. It may be it is these teachings that we read in her gospel – although some are more sceptical about this than I am.

---

[11] *The Gospel of Mary Magdalene*, translated by Jean-Yves Leloup, Inner Traditions, Rochester, Vermont, 2002, 25

[12] What are sometimes referred to as her seven sins or demons may also be the transformation by love of the seven manifestations of Wrath, referred to in Mary's gospel, which leads to Repose and Silence.

In any event, although, in the early years of Christendom, Mary's gospel was shunned and abandoned, reading her opening stanzas is, for us, both a revelation and a remembrance. It reveals that which we once knew but have forgotten – have been encouraged to forget. It takes us into a place of understanding that is both ancient and timeless, a place that, at some level, we have always known was there. It carries a resonance from a much earlier time, the time of the goddess Wisdom and the realm of the Moon.

This was a time when the divine presence was recognized to be, at one and the same time, both masculine and feminine. It was a time when this presence was known in the ever-changing rhythms of Nature, ebbing and flowing, and in the cycles and phases of the moon, arising, fullness, declining and darkness.[13] Often depicted with a skull, Mary Magdalene is associated with the third and declining phase of the moon, the phase that leads to the days of death and darkness, and then to resurrection or re-birth. The symbolism and meaning of this lunar tradition would have been understood in the lifetime of Jesus – the three Marys at the foot of the cross would have had a resonance with the Three Fates of Greek mythology, the weavers of shrouds whose thread determined the length of life;[14] the three dark days of the resurrection would signify the three dark days of the moon, which disappears before rising once again.

Each one of us will have our own view of these stories, but whether we like it or not there can be no doubt that the symbolism expressed in myth influences our understanding of the way things are. If it is not this myth that does so, it will be another. And it is at least possible that this particular myth of renewal, this timeless way of seeing and knowing, may be trying to be heard again in our time.

---

[13] Indeed, in this tradition, the name Magdalene is understood as meaning Great Moon – Magada "great" and "lene" lunar or of the moon. I am indebted to my fried Jules Cashford for this.

[14] Jules Cashford, *The Moon: Myth and Image*, Cassell Illustrated, 2003, 259-260.

I think it is. Indeed, I feel that it is there in an evermore urgent and insistent voice, to be heard at every place and time if we but have ears to hear.

But for this Wisdom to arise and be expressed, it has to be understood. And such understanding will not come from the modern quest for *explanation* but rather from our being as one who waits for *revelation* – a way of understanding that is difficult for us because we have forgotten how to do it, how to wait. For this reason alone, Mary's gospel is important to us, now, because it shows us something that we have lost but need – a more complete reality, a more cyclical and integrated reality:

> all the elements of Nature are interwoven
> and united with each other.[15]

Prefiguring the later teachings of Aquinas, to which we will come, Mary's gospel is also radical in that it sees Nature and our true nature as essentially good. Following on from the extract quoted above, Peter asks the Teacher a question:

> ... "Since you have become the interpreter
> of the elements and the events of the world, tell us:
> What is the sin of the world?"
> The Teacher answered:
> "There is no sin.
> It is you who make sin exist,
> when you act according to the habits
> of your corrupted nature;
> this is where sin lies."[16]

---

[15] *The Gospel of Mary Magdalene*, translated by Jean-Yves Leloup, Inner traditions, Rochester, Vermont, 2002, 25.

[16] Ibid, 25.

Here, then, we are asked to see – or rather behold – both an inherent goodness within the cosmos and that natural tendency towards goodness in all to which Thomas Aquinas would later refer. It is only when we fall from grace that our true nature is corrupted. And, as Mary Magdalene tells us, if we are able to shake off our blindness and ignorance so we become at one with that which truly is, we, too, will be, must needs be, part of this purposeful goodness. In this way, and only in this way, we will be fulfilled. Become One.

This is the teaching of Mary's gospel.

...then, Thomas Aquinas.

But if we want to discover how this might come about, we must now turn to Aquinas and his teaching of Natural Law, and, then, briefly, meet up with the mystic, Meister Eckhart.

The roots of Natural Law lie with the ancient Greeks, with Plato and Aristotle. The teachings then flourish with the Roman Stoics, with Cicero and Marcus Aurelius, and with the Neo-Platonist, Plotinus, before coming to Aquinas, who, in his *Summa Theologica*, sets the earlier teachings within a Christian context.[17]

According to Aquinas there is Eternal Law beyond and within the realm of Nature as we know it and experience it. This law governs all and does so not by will but by a natural and wholesome participation, which is ever moving all that is towards goodness and union with the Good, with God. This is the true nature of reality and

---

[17] The roots of these teachings can also be found in earlier times, for example in ancient Egypt, where the principles of harmony, balance and order are evident in the myths of the gods and the duties of the Pharaoh. See for example, Anne Baring and Jules Cashford, *The Myth of the Goddess: Evolution of an Image*, Viking Arkana, 1991.

we can *only* be truly ourselves when we act in accordance with it. Within Eternal Law, there is Natural Law, which is the manner in which we live when we live in a good and wholesome way; a way that enables us, in all we do, to be at one with that divine, lawful and eternal reality of which we are naturally a part. Love is the power holding us in this way of being and Providence is its guiding principle.

In all of this, says Aquinas, the special part played by humankind is our ability to reflect upon that which *is*. In doing this, we give expression to the inherent mindfulness or intelligence of Nature and its fulfilment in being truly known. Human lawfulness is therefore that which accords with the greater good of the whole – for the individual, society; for society, Nature; and for Nature, wholesome-ness and union with the Divine. Since we are part of both society and Nature then, to be truly ourselves, we needs must also participate towards their goodness and wholeness – which I would call "holiness".[18]

And then there is Providence, which is the essence of Natural Law, since it is the flowing stream into which we step in our participation with lawfulness. It is quite unlike predetermination, which, of course, expresses a sense of compulsion. In stepping into the unfolding stream of Providence, we choose to participate, *for when we do so we are most truly ourselves* and are naturally carried onwards towards the Good. Thus there is (and we by nature participate in) an intelligent, lawful and purposeful reality, ever moving towards wholeness and goodness. In the words of Aquinas:

> So all things tend through their movements
> and actions toward the divine likeness, as
> towards their ultimate end.[19]

---

[18] See David Cadman, *Holiness in the Everyday*, Quaker Books, 2009.
[19] Thomas Aquinas, *Summa Contra Gentiles*, Book 3 Part 1, 19.5, translated by Anton Pegis, 1973.

For me, this points towards a true way of being. And this is what I see when I look out of the window of my study and watch the ordered and regular movement of the seasons, the birth, life, death and rebirth of the garden.

I know, of course, that this reality of Aquinas has no meaning in the inert, mechanical, blind and purposeless universe of "enlightened" science, the reality of convention. It is, therefore, of no surprise that the consequences are as they are – no sense of the sacred, no true reverence for Nature, including all of humankind, and, thus, the disintegration of, and damage to, economies, environments and communities – and each one of us, too. Seen with the eye of Natural Law, it was inevitable that the irreversible and linear development of what I have now called "the old time" with its exclusive language of Reason and Enlightenment *alone*, would take us to where we are; that, unchallenged, it would run its course, step by step taking us further and further away from an understanding of that relationship and participation, which is now manifestly relevant to our time. But as we begin to see where it is we have been led to – the degradation of natural resources, the disruption of climate, the collapse of financial and economic structures, the loss of trust, and the widening gap between those who have and those who have not – it is also no surprise to find that in many millions of small ways many peoples (and more latterly governments) recognize a crisis of perception[20] and turn towards structures and processes that are integrative and whole.

In this, however, and especially at the level of government, it seems there is still a struggle to find the words needed to frame robust and sustainable policy and action. The old and profane language of

---

[20] For a discussion of this, see *Selected Speeches and Articles by His Royal Highness The Prince of Wales, Volume 2*, "*Harmony – a crisis of perception*", Editors David Cadman and Suheil Bushrui, The Center for Heritage Resource Studies, The University of Maryland, 2009.

separation and division has been so pervasive it stifles right thinking and expression. What is, therefore, needed is a new and I would say holy language – a rediscovery of Wisdom.

To find our way forward, we will, first, have to be prepared to re-align and clarify our perception of the way things are. We will have to find our way out of the constraints of separation and dis-integration – which have been set by "the old time" – and find our way into a new realm of reverence, connection, interdependence and wholeness. There was a time when to see the world in this way was commonplace. We have to bring such understanding back into our lives.

We often hear it said: "the end justifies the means". But in the tradition of Aquinas this would be a meaning-less thing to say, because the means, as it were, so often become the end. Indeed, it is worth noting what our Friend, William Penn, had to say about this:

A good end cannot sanctify evil means; nor
must we ever do evil that good may come of it...[21]

And, if we look once more at Natural Law, we find that it, too, emphasises the means, the "being with". Everything proceeds towards the Good only in as much as it participates in goodness itself, and is for the good of the whole. And such "providential order belongs to the nature of things":

---

[21] William Penn, *Quaker Faith and Practice*, 24.03.

The essential insight of Natural Law...is that there is a divine providential order in the cosmos, which draws all things ultimately to the Good. This providential order belongs to the nature of things as such and in this sense the cosmos is permeated by logos or reason.[22]

This "reason", however, does not, as we have been told for so long, emanate from the detached and observing individual towards an external cosmos. It is there "in the nature of things", to be received when we participate in it, when we turn ourselves towards it with a pure heart and mind. In this sense, to know what is true, we must learn to dwell with and in God, *to be with* God.

As I have already suggested, this way of being requires a completely different form of enquiry than the one we normally suppose to be true. Most of us have been brought up in a world in which we have been encouraged to seek for explanations; how is this made and how does this work? This is the modern form of enquiry, the way of the Reason and Enlightenment – and, of course, within its own limitations, it can be extremely useful and worthwhile. However, it is but one mode of thought and, given that its method has become centred so much upon the individual rather than the whole, it is at best limiting and at worst increasingly damaging.[23]

Natural Law offers us a different kind of "reason", one that is especially relevant for a society that calls itself The Religious Society of Friends:

---

[22] Joseph Milne, "All Things in the Mind of God and the Mind of God in all Things", *Eckhart Review* No.19, 2010.

[23] For a discussion on this see Joseph Milne, *Metaphysics and the Cosmic Order*, Temenos Academy, 2008.

This view of the cosmos, though "natural", is also essentially "religious". It is a religious way of apprehending reality. For the ancients this religious way of apprehending reality is understood as the primary way of apprehending reality, the way that transcends delusion or the fleeting images of mere appearances. It is the way the unity of reality is approached and apprehended. Thus, the more we say about it, the more it departs from our modern conceptions of the cosmos, and our modern conceptions of ultimate truth.[24]

All of us who acknowledge, or even wonder about, a spiritual dimension in our lives must surely, then, allow ourselves to participate in a different form of enquiry. In this form, there is no end to which we progress, only good being and being that is not good. And if we struggle with this it may be, in part, because our modern mode of perception – knowing by external observation – clouds our ability to see things as they are in and of themselves. We only have one way of knowing or believing. And because of this we are blinded to any other possibility. Indeed it is as if such another possibility must be unreal.

But here comes Meister Eckhart, for he has something shocking to say about the way in which we come to "know". Our modern way, which is markedly possessive, assumes that we get to know something by bringing our reason to bear upon an otherwise unknown "thing"; we take it apart and through our own intelligence make it known. For Eckhart, this is all the wrong way round. Things only exist and are knowable because they are already known by God. If being precedes action, knowing precedes being. Everything that has been and is, is known; its origin or beginning arises simultaneously with its being known. At best, we participate and receive:

---

[24] Joseph Milne, "All Things in the Mind of God and the Mind of God in all Things", *Eckhart Review* No.19, 2010.

Modern secular thought has become so accustomed to assuming that the human intellect is the only knowing agent in the cosmos that it is a great challenge to consider that our knowledge of things may come from a universal primary knowledge that holds things in existence, that the cosmos is essentially an act of knowledge, or that knowledge is prior to the being of things and their principle. This turns our usual epistemology upside-down.[25]

Difficult though this is for us, we have to let go of the desire – the compulsion – to govern our knowing *only* with the external observation of a supposedly rational mind and allow what is already true to be shown to us within. This requires a contemplative and receptive mode of being.

So, once again, to think about what it means to "be Quaker", or indeed to contemplate any future way of being, we have to come to know what it means "to be". And to do this we have to peel back the obscuring layers that have come to diminish our capacity to see clearly – to behold. To begin with, we have to see conventional modes of thought for what they are – no more than one way of seeing the world. Then we have to allow a more complete and integrated vision of the world to come forth; allowing our narrow reason to broaden out and embrace older and timeless ways of knowing. We have to set aside the present possessive and self-centred ways for a way of knowing that can only be experienced in

---

[25] Ibid. Milne goes on to say: "Nevertheless, Eckhart is following Aquinas here, and not simply because of his Platonic tendencies but because it is the primacy of the act of knowing in God which for Eckhart provides the key to how created things are at once within God and yet come forth from God."

participation with and waiting upon the Divine. Most importantly, we have to allow means to take us towards ends.

The Whole is One. And until we see and know this truly, we will continue to be fettered by what is now an outmoded perception – one that is too narrow, too materialistic, too self-centred, too assertive to enable us to understand things as they really are. For Quakers, and perhaps for others, this means recognizing the importance of a practical and nurturing mysticism over and above mere "busyness". And, whether or not we are Quakers, we have to rediscover the common place, the contemplative, the integrative, the self-less, the gentle, the generous dwelling-in and being-with one another, Nature and the Divine. Only in this will we be able to find the way forward.

A Way of Surrender

Drop Thy still dews of quietness,
Till all our strivings cease;
Take from our souls the strain and stress,
And let our ordered lives confess
The beauty of Thy peace.

John Greenleaf Whittier.

Letting go of anxious mind – the restless quest to put everything in order with "me" at the centre – there is ease; surrendering to the Great Mystery, which gathers me in, there is peace – at-one-ment.

When the Buddha awakened from his deep meditation beneath the Bhodi Tree, he spoke of what he had seen – the rising and falling away of life birth and death; "Coming to be, coming to be! Ceasing to be, ceasing to be!". At every place, in every moment however long or short, this is what is happening. And the holy life of the everyday – the life that is common and whole – is found in such daily surrender, by the letting go of self. This we must learn. For in the end we will all have to surrender. At some time, and for each one of us, life in this world will end and our bodies will be given back to the earth or the air, leaving our souls to find their way home.

So much of my life has been taken up with what I thought had to be done – to study, to work, to "succeed". Often this has meant that my attention has been distracted, driven by ignorance and stupidity, by vanity and foolishness. And so it is I have searched outside for what was always there, inside; struggling when I should have surrendered.

But now I see more clearly what it is I must do. Dadi Janki of the Brahma Kumaris says: "The more you practice taking spiritual light and might from God, the lighter you will feel internally as this becomes your spiritual state of being. You will also experience yourself to be a divine point of light". I listen to what she says for she is wise.

So, as our quest continues, let us return once more to Aquinas and his Natural Law.

In the Spring and Summer of 2009, I studied a series a papers written by Joseph Milne – from whose writings I have already quoted.[26] In these papers, Joseph suggested that, according to Natural Law, every part of Nature has a tendency towards fulfilment; an inclination to become the best of whatever it is and of whatever it can be, thereby offering itself for the good of Nature as a whole. It is natural for the part to nurture the whole, just as the hand takes the blow aimed at the body or a mother gives herself for her children. And, as conscious beings, it is our role to know things for what they truly are so that all may be known and come "to rest"[27] – to be at one with the presence of the Divine, which knows all, and which some of us call God. Thus, we must play our part. In reverence, we must submit ourselves to the common and greater good of the whole and thus, and only thus, find rest and peace.[28]

---

[26] The papers started with one given at Manchester Metropolitan University , September 2008 on *Religion and Political Theory and Philosophy*. The paper, which has not been published was entitled "Society and Natural Law in Thomas Aquinas".

[27] From a private conversation with Joseph Milne 31st March 2009

[28] Ibid.

As we have already seen, Joseph explains how in the thirteenth century, in the teachings of Thomas Aquinas, creation came to be understood as being "not only good but also rational and intelligible"; that "Nature was intelligent and oriented towards the maximum fullness of being and reason at all levels".[29] According to this Law, the natural world works by way of an impulse (a relationship) both from and towards what is Good and Whole, "reconciling the realm of Nature with the realm of Grace".[30] By starting from the premise that the created world directly manifests the divine wisdom of God, it thus provides us with a new and quite different insight into how we might consider our relationship with Nature – a different set of principles to govern such a relationship.

In the search for a way of being, this is a great help. For seeing the natural world as the revelation of "the divine Wisdom of God"[31], seeing it as good and lawful and as the inevitable expression of divine cause, goes to the root of our relationships with each other and with the rest of Nature. And it places upon all of us a very particular responsibility as we wrestle to come to terms with the economic and environmental damage we have caused by our own thoughtlessness and profligacy.

We are part of a greater whole and this requires us to situate ourselves within, *surrender ourselves to*, this natural order as part of an essential inclination towards the fullness of being and goodness. It means that understanding our potential destiny depends upon a truthful correspondence with Nature, and thus with Natural Law.[32]

---

[29] Joseph Milne, "Society and Natural Law in Thomas Aquinas", a paper given at a *Religion and Political Theory and Philosophy* Conference, Manchester Metropolitan University, September 2008, unpublished.

[30] Ibid.

[31] Ibid.

[32] Ibid.

In the light of this, I have now come to see the matter of my life and death in a different way. When I see a thrush pulling a worm from the ground, do I see an act of violence or sacrifice? For whether I like it or not, I, too, sacrifice my body day and night to minute, microscopic organisms that feed upon me; and when I die my body – flesh, bones and tissues – will return to Nature. What is important is whether we give or take each of these acts of mutuality and reciprocity with a sense of thankfulness, true understanding and humility or whether we resist them; whether or not we surrender and behold in this the work of Love.

This may sound at odds with all that we see around and about us but in the end we find what we are looking for. If we expect to find a world of violence – red in tooth and claw, the worm torn from the ground – then we shall. But if we open our eyes to the wonder and goodness of the world, we will find that, too. In this sense, what is good is that which properly plays its part for the good of the whole; and the bad is the reverse of this.

By surrendering the self, we come to see that our true nature is neither inherently bad nor good. At root, to act well does not lie in the realm of ethics but in the realm of truth, of true being. To act badly is to act otherwise than in accordance with our true nature, otherwise than in accordance with Natural Law. And when we do this we are without grace, we act grace-less-ly, not by way of judgment but by way of being. It is not a matter of morality but a matter of revelation.

It is by attentive experience and waiting that we find our way. The Buddha described this in terms of whether or not we are "skilful", whether we learn from experience. And on one occasion when asked about how we could know the true way he replied:

Do not go by oral tradition, by lineage of teaching, by hearsay, by a collection of scriptures, by logical reasoning, by inferential reasoning, by reflection on reasons, by the acceptance of a view by pondering it, by the seeming competence of a speaker, or because you think, "The ascetic is our teacher". But when you know for yourselves, "These things are unwholesome, these things are blameable; these things are censured by the wise; these things, if undertaken and practiced, lead to harm and suffering", then you should abandon them.[33]

According to Aquinas, this orientation towards the good is the essential nature of all that is.[34] In created things, good is found not only as regards their substance but also as regards their order towards an end, especially their last end, which is divine goodness.[35] The constant and providential unfolding of Nature is eternal and good and we are a part of it *and we needs must surrender to it.*

The notion that Nature is intelligent and purposeful seems to me to be likely to be true. For when I look at Nature I see rhythm, pattern and order. Order implies purpose and purpose implies mind or intelligence. That Nature is intelligent seems self-evident and in accordance with my experience – albeit there are always obstacles and, time and again, they cause us to break with the order of Being.

Until quite recently, one of the obstacles to my own surrender was the very word "God". Like others, perhaps, I had allowed an intellectual and to some extent emotional concern with meaning and form to hamper me. But then, one morning in my local Meeting, it came to me to stop worrying about it. I did and immediately

---

[33] J Nyaponika Thera and Bhikkhu Bodhi, *Numerical Discourses of the Buddha: An Anthology of Suttas from the Anguttara Nikyna*, Vistaar Publications, New Delhi, 2000, 65.

[34] Joseph Milne, *The Providential Order of the Universe*, a lecture given to The Temenos Academy 8th June 2009, unpublished.

[35] Ibid.

I was filled with great peace. I think what may have triggered this surrender was a story I had heard[36] about a class of primary school children who were taking part in a drawing class. One little girl of six was especially absorbed in her drawing. The teacher asked her what she was drawing, to which the little girl replied, "I am drawing God". "But," said the teacher, "no-one knows what God looks like". To which the child replied, "They will do when I've finished my drawing".

Letting go of worrying about "God", accepting the word for what it is, ceasing to fret about this Great Mystery – which, by definition, is beyond explanation – has enabled me to bring the word back into my discourse and prayers in such a way that all sorts of doors open themselves. The indwelling of God now arises without hindrance, and I begin to move more easily into a place of knowing that is beyond the mere human intellect, the place that Meister Eckhart and other mystics speak of when they talk of us knowing ourselves in the mind of God. It is a great relief to be no longer alone, trying to work it all out on my own. Now I simply open my heart to the presence of God and rest there. I wait on God with as pure a heart as I can.

Such a form of surrender requires a complete absence of Western cynicism. Beyond all the mechanics of life, it requires us to surrender our rational mind to the intellect of the heart. Unless we are able to do this, we will always be operating and seeking within the limits of a world we have made for ourselves. Despite its evident limits, we will never be able to transcend that world. And yet, either personally or corporately, if we are really going to be able to find new ways forward, in the "still dews of quietness" as Whittier puts is, we will have to loosen ourselves from such fetters and open our hearts and minds to the Goodness of God.

---

[36] A video by Ken Robinson on www.ted.com

In his book *A Testament of Devotion*, and writing in the first half of the twentieth century, the American Quaker, Thomas Kelly, talks about a surrender to the inner sanctuary of the soul, a Divine Centre:

> Deep within us all there is an amazing inner sanctuary of the soul, a holy place, a Divine Centre, a speaking Voice, to which we may continuously return. Eternity is at our hearts, pressing on our time-torn lives, warming us with intimations of an astounding destiny, calling us home unto Itself.[37]

For Thomas Kelly, it was necessary for us to question the busyness of our lives, not to withdraw from action but to ensure first that we have attended to our inner lives; that we first centre down "and live in that holy Silence that is dearer than life".[38] Ensuring that whatever it is that we then, and only then, do arises from and out of Divine Presence. Such a life is founded in constant silent prayer, humility and a divine attendance. Such a life is a revolution.

---

[37] Thomas R. Kelly, *A Testament of Devotion*, Harper San Francisco, 1941, 3.
[38] Ibid, 95.

Finding Our Way?

"Take heed, dear Friends, to the promptings of love and truth in your hearts. ... Bring the whole of your life under the ordering of the spirit of Christ. ... Seek to know an inward stillness..."

Extracts from Advices and Queries 1-3.

As Quakers, we are open to teaching but not inclined to receive it without question. Collectively and alone, we believe we must find our own way to God by waiting upon His presence. In bringing the teachings of others to bear upon our own concern, we need, attentively and with humility, to test them by our own reflection and experience until we know them to be true. This is our tradition, our way. Working within this tradition, we, surely, need to feel that teachings speak to us in truth. As best we can, and with all our own frailties, we have to listen with a discerning but open heart and find whether or not we are truly guided by them. I am sure there are many others who feel the same. And I am convinced that, in this, the relentless working of a busy and grasping mind will not be enough – and may even be a hindrance. Quakers or not, our discernment has to be of another order, something almost impossible to describe but nonetheless knowable. We need to behold rather than see. For revelation rather than explanation is our mystical path, a path of knowing through being true and waiting – the promptings of love and truth in our hearts.

When I read *The Gospel of Mary Magdelene* or study the Natural Law of Thomas Aquinas, I feel at one with what they tell. They make sense to me and they relate to my own experience. In a way, they are even familiar. Together, they seem to say: all that is is interconnected and united with the One; there is an order and purpose in our lives, which draws us towards the goodness of the whole; we are most ourselves when we participate in this goodness, letting go of selfishness and surrendering to the working of Divine Love; it is Love that unites and draws us towards the Good, towards God. Our task is not to define our destination but to surrender, wait and then walk aright. This is our way of being.

I am writing this as the Summer has given way to the first days of Autumn. My body feels the change of temperature; my eyes notice the softness of the light and the shortening of days. Everything around me is becoming Autumn, not least the trees whose leaves are turning yellow, orange and deep red, dropping one by one onto the ground. The swallows have gone and the garden birds who will share the Winter with us are left behind. The soldier plants are slowly sinking to the bottom of the pond; there are spiders everywhere; and the toad finds a home in the compost box. I, too, am slowing down, wearing warmer clothes – as it were, drawing inwards.

These natural events feel True and they feel Good, of God. They are an expression of Divine Beauty. When I let myself follow my natural feelings and surrender to the turning of the year, I am at one; I know I am acting aright; I feel the presence of Divine Love giving shape not only to me but to all that is around me.

What, then, does this say about a "way of being", and the ways in which we might come to understand one of the most compelling problems of our time – that addiction to economic growth to which I referred my Introduction?

Let's start from where we are. At the end of this first decade of the second millennium, we find ourselves in some distress and disarray. We find ourselves living through a period of great financial and economic disruption. We have seen banks all but collapse and economies falling into recession, only to be "rescued" by the kind of state support that would have been impossible to imagine before it happened. Once again, those with least suffer the most, and it is clear that government expenditure, which was the sticking plaster used to stop the immediate bleeding, cannot be sustained. Indeed it is already being cut back. At the same time, post Copenhagen 2009, we continue to face the threat of climate change and resource depletion. For some, midst flood and drought, this is no longer a threat but an awful reality.

We are living in a period not simply of change but of transformation – an old world is giving place to a new realm. In ancient myth, the possibility of such change was understood and told in many stories, not least in the story of the sons of Zeus, Apollo and Dionysus, where, to enable renewal to take place, the order of Apollo is disrupted by the chaos of Dionysus. In our own mythology, the tale is the same: the maker of change, the one who turns the wheel of life, the "shift-shaper" is the Old Woman who, in the dark half of the year, enables the seeds of Autumn to be transformed into the green shoots of Spring, where she will appear as the Maiden and, later, in times of harvest, as the Queen. The wheel of the year must turn.[39] Transformation will have its way. Therefore, however much we may long for stasis, the truth is that all is (has to be) in flux.

---

[39] See, for example, David Cadman, *The King Who Lost His Memory* available from www.zigpublishing.com

The change we are now experiencing may not be the regular rhythm of change seen in markets, as fluctuations of greater and lesser prosperity arise around some supposed equilibrium. It may well be something of greater volatility and magnitude that will greatly affect society, economy and environment. Nevertheless, what may at one moment appear to be collapse and disorder may also be part of a necessary wave of change, which in destroying leads to renewal – the story of Apollo and Dionysus. And so, we can only find our way forward in transformation. Mindful though we might be (must be) of eternal truth, there is little to be gained from trying to hold onto old and outworn rigidities. The questions we have to ask are therefore: What was it about the old time that needed to be destroyed in order that a new and more harmonious realm can arise? What should remain and what should go? Where is this destructive/creative wave of transformation trying to take us? How can we best ride the wave?

From all that is happening, we can see that the old world that we are leaving was deeply flawed; the difficulties it has brought about are not an unfortunate and inexplicable accident but are a direct consequence of the values and principles upon which it had come to depend – too disconnected, too materialistic, too greedy, too self-centred, too violent and, I would say, too prosaic and too godless. Seeking a new realm will require new forms of perception and a new language in which that perception can be expressed. The old and flawed language of convention – the language of selfishness, acquisitiveness and institutionalised greed – and its supposed but narrow rationality is not an option because it will simply bring us back to where we are.

However difficult it might be, what is needed is the re-birth of a way of being rooted in, and expressive of, the perennial or timeless wisdom which lies at the root of all of the great spiritual traditions and which was, of course, taught in the parables of Jesus and his sermon on the mount – meekness, simplicity, peacefulness, generosity of spirit, forgiveness and justice; truths of integration, wholeness and self-less-ness. However difficult this may be, however unrealistic it may at first sound (and there will be many who say it is), it is no more complicated than this and we should not be persuaded that it is. We do not have to find something which has never been known before but, since we have lost our way, we do have to rediscover it. It is this (and only this) wisdom of wholeness, participation and integration, which will be able to provide our foothold. The chances are that the new realm towards which we are moving will be fraught with difficulty – a shortage of resources, a hostile climate, a population too large to be sustained, great inequalities and injustice, significant insecurity, anger and hatred – but these are the very conditions which require a new way of being. This is the challenge we face.

And what is it we as Quakers can offer? Fond as I am of my fellow Quakers and convinced as I am that, together, we have a contribution to make, I am sometimes conscious of our complacency. The very fact we are so often liked, even admired, by others for our supposed tolerance and "good works" can make us overly self-satisfied or spiritually complacent. It can make us assume we have already found the right way of being at the very time when we need to challenge ourselves individually and corporately. This must, surely, be one of those times. Nevertheless, I want to suggest that in all of this, we must, at the same time, have confidence in those parts of our tradition that have served us well. Indeed, we should deepen this experience and not be "hurried" into ways that take us away from this. Whilst we should never be afraid of the need for change, my suggestion is that one of the most important things we need is ever to slow down and to insist upon reflection before action.

There has never been a time when this was more true. Although, therefore, many of the problems we have to face up to are urgent, the starting point for action must always be our Meetings for Worship and our blessed stillness and silence. Whenever we gather together, locally, regionally or nationally, we must continue to begin by bringing ourselves into the presence of the Divine and to do this for as long as it takes us to find our centre. Only from this point can we hope to find true action. This should never be hurried, and curbing our (or at least my) natural impatience should be an essential part of our personal and corporate governance.

We must learn to dwell in thought in such a way that we are ever mindful of an essential interconnectedness. Above all else, the problems we face show a need for an understanding of "related-ness", the ways in which the economic, the social and the environmental are, in the words of Mary's gospel, "interwoven and united" with each other. In doing this, the structure and character of Aquinas's Natural Law helps us to see that above all else we act most truly when we act for the goodness of the whole – the economy as a whole, the community as a whole, an ecosystem as a whole.

Perhaps, we can make this a special part of the way in which we contribute to the debate about these matters and the ways in which programmes of action are arrived at – "holding spaces"[40] for listening not only to what others have to say but what can be heard of the divine voice. Perhaps, because of our naturally contemplative way of being and our love of stillness and silence, we can make it our special task to understand and hold this whole-some-ness (or, as I would call it, holiness) and offer a particular and evident place for it to be expressed in prayerful community. Our record on peace and social concern stands as a strong foundation. Now we need to bring such

---

[40] Linda Murgatroyd, "The future of Quakers in Britain: holding spaces for the spirit to act", *The Friends Quarterly*, 2010.

concerns within the wider ambit of what we have come to know as "sustainability" – the eternal goodness of the whole. There will be many others who are at the same place and we can share this work with them.

There is then the matter of justice. Many of us in the North, together and alone, are already living at levels of consumption and expectation that take us beyond the carrying capacity of the Earth.[41] Those who have most must therefore give to those who have least. Politicians cannot say this. But it is the truth nonetheless. Many of us and many of our children and grandchildren will need to see the "quantities" (but not necessarily the "qualities") of our lives being reduced, either by choice or by compulsion. The discomfort this will bring to us, matched by the growing despair of those who have least, will test us. Without the strong foundation of Love, which governs all, there will be great disturbance and unrest. As the "dogma of consumption" falls apart, what will hold us together? Without the governance of Love, what will guide us? In every way, as we meet together and with others, can we be exemplars of this Love in action?

This is the context in which we can discern what it means to be Quaker and to discover what our particular contribution can be. Many of our reputed characteristics – a love of simplicity, a concern for others, our testimony of peace and self-discipline, our tolerance of others – will serve us well. But most important of all will be our ways of proceeding. Indeed, part of my testimony, such as it is, is to propose that if we proceed aright then the "ends", our futures, will be as they will be; our futures will arise from the ways in which we take steps towards them. In this, therefore, I have only these suggestions: ever mindful of the timeless teachings of our tradition,

---

[41] See: Donella H. Meadows, Jorgen Randers, Dennis L. Meadows, *Limits to Growth: The 30-Year Update*, Chelsea Green Publishing Company, 2004.

we break free of the fetters of "the old world"; we strengthen our simplicity; we nurture our compassion; and we remember we must always be asking the question: who is my neighbour. And, finally, in all of this and in the words of William Penn, "Let us then try what Love will do".[42]

---

[42] William Penn, *Quaker Faith and Practice*, 24.03

Epilogue

From the very beginning, and inspired most especially by verses from *The Gospel of Mary Magdalene*, I have been directed by a profound sense of interconnection and interdependence – a sense that the mundane and the divine are one and inseparable.

If these two realms appear apart, this is only because we have been taught to make a false distinction between the two. We may not even have been inclined to make such a distinction but we have learnt to do so. Where there is only one realm, convention requires that we see two – the one practical and the other mystical. To see that this cannot be so, let me, finally, take one or two of the mundane propositions of "limits to growth" and see how they *needs must dwell within* a divine way of being.

As a start, consider the very root of our economic conventions, a set of propositions which, whether we are conscious of them or not, shape our lives. If we are going to be able to do anything at all to prevent the kinds of distress to which these propositions have led us, we need to see them for what they are. Otherwise, in our passive ignorance, they will continue unchallenged and unabated.

At the core of our present Western economy is the notion of conflict. Businesses, we are told, only succeed by forceful competition with each other. Those that work for them are encouraged by a mixture of carrots and sticks, as if they were donkeys – on the one hand bonuses for successful performance and on the other the fear of dismissal for failure. Using the language of the battlefield, businesses want their staff to lose their own identity in that of the company as if they were part of a single battalion of troopers fighting for success. Secrecy and control are often thought to be essential.

And yet, my own experience of setting up and developing businesses that have worked well tells me that this is not only a very singular and particular convention but also one that is mightily flawed. Contrary to the orthodoxy of suspicion and competition, I have found that successful business ventures *depend upon* deep levels of trust and co-operation. Above all else, they require a sense of shared purpose in which an obsession with profitability is not allowed to constrain imagination and creativity. Profit arises from good work well done and not the other way around.

In my experience, to work well and with commitment, we need to feel not only a shared purpose but also an open-ness and honesty of endeavour in which both strengths and weaknesses can be discussed without fear. Fear destroys. The vital qualities of "enthusiasm" and "inspiration" both come from the Greek "*entheos*" or god inspired – their root being grounded in the divine. Over and over again, I have experienced how such enthusiasm enables people to fulfil themselves, often freely giving more than has been asked of them. And at the same time I have seen how fear and control can cause people to wither away, resenting their work and all that is demanded of them.

However, I also know that to even begin to contemplate and suggest such a proposition requires us to challenge convention, and to do this we have radically to realign our perceptions. This is why my testimony on a way of being becomes not just some kind of unreal and intellectual indulgence but an essential form of work, preparing the ground for action.

By way of another example, take the underlying proposition of "limits to growth", which is that despite our capacity for innovation we have to accept that, within a finite planet and mindful of the needs of others, there must be a limit to our own consumption. This is difficult to accept within present conventions – as can be seen from the fact that all of those that lead us continue to underscore the need for unlimited "growth". Unable to envisage the possibility of our accepting restraint, they feel the need to offer "growth" as the driver for satisfying what they assume to be our insatiable appetites. Despite the evidence of its adverse consequences, "growth" becomes the cure-all: it will provide jobs; it will enable us to fund hospitals and schools; it will even deliver a safer society.

But the truth is that without a change in this convention we shall continue to be led to catastrophe. So how do we make such a change if the only language we can use is the very one that has led us to where we are? The answer is we have to change our language. This can only be done of we change our way of being. And the ground for this can only be found in teachings that lie outwith mundane convention – teachings that arise from within the realm of divine discourse. We cannot change future outcomes by using the old language. We cannot find new ways of being by following old and outmoded ways. We have to change, surrender and change.

It is only when we see and accept that our purpose is not self-centred but is to fit into a divine purpose of fulfilment that we can see what this change must be: to understand that our own needs and wants must be, can only be, set *in relation to* the good of the whole. And, Quakers or not, this understanding arises not from busyness alone but from a reflection and prayer that leads to true and sustained action. We *have* to dwell in stillness and silence in order to be able to find our way. Otherwise we shall continue to be swept along in modes of thought and being which are calamitous. True action can *only* arise from true reflection.

Finally, we have to give urgent attention to our relationship with those people distant from ourselves who are going to be most disastrously affected by climate change. Again, my suggestion is that we cannot truly understand our responsibility in this in terms of a convention or language of separateness. Indeed, I suggest we cannot understand what needs to de done until and unless we feel ourselves to be part of their families. If these programmes are to be sustained, so that they are effective, this will require a commitment to practical programmes to foster, nurture and help these distant neighbours. Quakers or not, we have to bring all of our resources to bear – hearts and minds.

In the preparation of this testimony, I spoke to someone at Friends House who had responsibility for work with families in Africa and I understood from her that it was not just about funding – although this is important – but also about providing support in tenderness and prayer for all who represent us in this work. And we need to do this not because we are "nice people" but because we are inextricably connected in spirit with what they do. They need this support, too. Unless we can become entirely attached to their work in both our minds and our hearts, it will not flourish; it will be what someone else is doing and what we are, at best, paying for. Too much distance.[43]

And so my testimony is that the problems we are about to face are of such a dimension that present convention is entirely unacceptable. It will not do. I am not sure how this change can come about or what it would mean for each one of us if it did, but I am utterly convinced that it requires a radical change of heart and being. This will only come about when we disrupt our complacency and find new ways of being that acknowledge our interdependence not as an idea but as a way of life. This requires such a momentous shift in our perception it can only be brought about by an act of mystical transformation, an act of deliberate surrender, a new way of being.

---

[43] David Cadman, "Just Being", *Quaker Voices, Vol. 6*, November 2010.

Other recent publications by David Cadman

Holiness in the Everyday
Holiness in the Everyday brings together for the first time a group of essays on topics such as peace, sustainability and love that have been at the heart of the author's writings for the last ten or so years. The essays are set within the context of Quaker testimony, that is the way in which Quakers express their faith both in their meetings for worship and in their everyday lives. Most especially, the book seeks to bring back into our lives wholeness and holiness.

Holiness in the Everyday can be ordered from Quaker Books, Friends House, 173-177 Euston Road, London, NW1 2BJ
(020 7663 1030)
Cost: £7.00

The Roots of Sustainability
The Roots of Sustainability probes beneath and beyond the conventional discussion of sustainability to reveal that upon which it depends.

The Roots of Sustainability is available from:
Ben Bolgar
The Prince's Foundation
19-22 Charlotte Road
Shoreditch
London
EC2A 3SG
Cost: £13.50 inc. p&p

FSC
Mixed Sources
Product group from well-managed forests and other controlled sources
Cert no. TT-COC-003052
www.fsc.org
© 1996 Forest Stewardship Council

More of David's work can be found at
www.zigpublishing.com